Airport Strategic Planning

The fundamental concept of learning Airport Strategic Planning is to grasp how airports function effectively.

Davalsab.M.L

Author

Airport Strategic Planning

© 2023 by Davalsab.M.L

ISBN: 9798864441213 (Amazon)

About This subject

In this subject, we will look at airport strategic planning. We will look at how airports are developed and what factors influence airport construction.

Airport strategic planning and construction involves carefully mapping out the future of an airport. It considers factors like passenger needs and air traffic trends to upgrade facilities, runways, and services. It's essential for the airport's growth and efficiency, requiring collaboration among stakeholders for safe and sustainable development.

What you'll learn in this course:

- We will look at airport classifications and airfield components.
- The Space Relationships and Area Requirement Factors for Airline Decision and Other Airport Operations
- The terminology used in the construction of Runway Intersections, Taxiways, Clearances, Aprons, and Holding Apron.
- Airport Characteristics Numbering Related to Airport Design

CONTENTS

AIRPORT STRATEGIC PLANNING

Airport strategic planning is a comprehensive and organized process that focuses on setting long-term goals and objectives for an airport. This blueprint guides the expansion, renovation, and enhancement of airport facilities, runways, terminals, and services to meet future needs, improve efficiency, and enhance the passenger experience.

CHAPTER 1

1.1 INTRODUCTION

Most modes of transportation have their own importance. For example, the railway has its own station where all of the operations' facilities are laid out, and ships have their own connecting surface from water to land. Similarly, aircraft have their own operational site, which is known as an airport. To operate an aeroplane, a proper runway, a parking place for passengers, and a specific site for the aircraft to be stored are all required.

The central hub for an airline's operations is the airport, which primarily facilitates commercial air travel. An airport typically comprises a landing area, providing an accessible open space with at least one functional surface, like a runway for aircraft take-offs and landings, or a helipad. Additionally, airports often encompass various supporting structures such as control towers, hangars, and terminals, serving the purpose of aircraft maintenance and monitoring.

Larger airports further feature amenities such as aprons, taxiway bridges, air traffic control centres, and passenger facilities, including restaurants and lounges. Additionally, they are equipped with emergency services. In some countries, like the United States, airports may also host one or more fixed-base operators catering to general aviation needs.

1.2 Air Transport

We first learned about the importance of air transportation in the beginning of the classes. It is one of the world's fastest modes of transportation. It aids the majority of people, travellers, and businesses in maintaining their operations.

Air travel is one of the quickest ways of public transit for crossing international borders. Air travel allows people from many countries to cross international borders for personal, commercial, medical, and tourism reasons. Although air travel is the quickest mode of transportation due to the reduced flight duration, another benefit is the passenger amenities and level of comfort.

Spice Jet, Indigo Carriers, and Air India are among the many airlines available. The airline industry is currently experiencing intense competition. Each firm provides a variety of perks to tempt travellers. The primary purpose is to boost profits. It used to be tough to figure out what passengers wanted and needed. Airlines provide the majority of services from the highest level of care in order to provide passengers with a better travel experience.

The airport also plays an important role in providing aircraft facilities. Passengers use social media to provide feedback, which helps airlines improve their services. This information sharing has a substantial impact on the airline industry's competitiveness. It also enables them to improve their services and amenities for international travellers.

Aircraft play an important part in air transportation by transporting passengers. As a result, the flight is divided into three sections. There are flights available for short, medium, and long distances. Airlines will choose aircraft based on the required distance of the trip. When it comes to picking planes for their customers, airlines have their own preferences.

1.3 Growth of Air Transport

Every year, the need for air travel increases. The most crucial factor is accessibility. Many countries rely on air transportation for speedy access. Countries are working to develop their tourist sectors in order to attract more international visitors. The aviation industry is not only restricted to passengers; cargo transportation is also in high demand. During the COVID 19 outbreak, numerous airlines played a critical role in transporting vaccine from one country to another, and the rise in e-commerce is helping to propel airlines to new heights. Passenger airlines can now transport both passengers and cargo within range.

The aviation sector is growing quickly and will continue to do so in the future. Air travel demand is expected to expand at a rate of 4.3 percent per year over the next 20 years, according to current projections.

The air transportation industry will offer 15.5 million direct jobs and $1.5 trillion in global GDP if current growth rates are maintained through 2036. When the effects of worldwide tourism are included in, these statistics might rise to 97.8 million jobs and $5.7 trillion in GDP.

By the mid-2030s, 200,000 aircraft per day are expected to take off and land around the world. The amount of air traffic surprises some individuals. Around the world, planes are departing at about 400 per hour - and that's just scheduled commercial travel.

Sharing and using technology and best practises from aviation and all modes of transportation will aid the expanding mobility sector's performance and long-term viability by fostering public trust and ensuring long-term viability.

In 2017, planes transported about 4.1 billion people around the world. They flew 37 million commercial flights and transported 56 million tonnes of freight. Every day, airlines transport about 10 million passengers and almost USD 18 billion in freight.

DID YOU KNOW?

Since 1998, Hartsfield-Jackson Atlantic International Airport has been the world's busiest passenger airport. There are five runways. With a height of 121 metres, it was North America's and the world's fourth tallest air traffic control tower. 80 percent of the US commercial population is within a two-hour flight of the airport.

1.4 Classifications of Airports and Airfield Components

The term "Airport" has a specific meaning, and it isn't just a place where planes land. It also includes all of the infrastructure and facilities. The distinction is made, according to the FAA, because of the sort of activity undertaken at the airport and the frequency of arrivals and departures.

The functions and processes of the airport are classified.

1. International Airport
2. Domestic airport
3. Regional Airport
4. Basic Airport

International Airport:

National and International flights are served by this type of airport. The airport may have all of the necessary amenities to meet international standards. It serves as the country's entry point because it will be equipped with high security and a customs agency. It can operate a wide range of aircraft, from small to large.

Domestic Airport

These airports are Regional economies that benefit from connecting big cities and villages to regional and national markets. They are mostly found in urban areas and serve relatively large populations. Metropolitan Statistical Areas having a core urban population of at least 5, 00,000 people or Metropolitan Statistical Areas with a core urban population of 10,000 to 50,000 people can host regional airports.

Regional Airport

State or surrounding area Local airports are usually found near bigger population centres, however, they are not always found in metropolitan or metropolitan areas. The majority of flying at local airports is done by piston aircraft for business and personal reasons. Flight instruction, emergency services, and charter passenger services are common at these airports. These airport facilities are also useful for connecting holy sites and tourism areas with fewer flights each day.

Basic Airport

By connecting the neighbourhood to the national airport system, this sort of airport supports general aviation activities such as emergency response, air ambulance service, flight training, and personal flying. For business and personal reasons, the majority of flying at small airports is done by self-piloted propeller-driven aircraft. They typically carry out their responsibilities with only a single runway or helipad and minimal infrastructure.

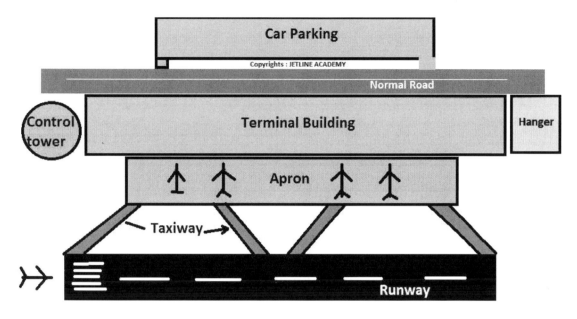

Airfield Components

1.5 Airfield Components

1. **Runway**: A runway is a constructed land strip used for aircraft landing and take-off. It is in a flat place with no obstructions in its path. Special markers are used to distinguish the runway from other roads.

2. **Taxiway**: The taxiway connects the terminal area, apron, and hanger to either end of the runway, among other things. These, like runways, are made of asphalt or concrete. It enables planes to transition from one runway to the next with ease.

3. **Apron:** An apron is a plane parking place. It's also where planes are loaded and unloaded. An apron is a paved area in front of the terminal building or near the hangers. The size and kind of apron are typically determined by the number of aircraft expected at the airport.

4. **Terminal building**: Airport administrative functions are offered in the terminal building. In this structure, passengers are examined

before and after their journeys. Lounges, cafes, and other amenities are available to passengers. Through sky bridges, walkways, and other means, passengers can enter the plane straight from terminal buildings.

5. **Control tower**: An airport's control tower is essential because it updates pilots and other ground crew members on the status of the aircraft. A location where aircraft, whether on the ground or in the air, in a certain zone are controlled.

   The controller uses radars to observe the situation, and information is transmitted by radio. The control tower controller monitors all aircraft in that zone and tells pilots on airport traffic, landing routes, visibility, wind speeds, runway data, and other pertinent information.

6. **Hanger:** It is the location where the majority of the facilities for repairing and servicing aircraft are done. It has the capacity to hold aircraft. The taxiway connects the hanger with the runway, allowing an aircraft to be quickly relocated to the hanger for repairs. Steel trusses and frames are used to construct it in the shape of a huge shed.

7. **Parking:** This is a location outside the terminal building or occasionally under the ground of the terminal building where airport workers or guests can store their automobiles.

1.6 Airport Organizations

Airports are crucial places for airline operations, and a strong policy framework is needed to keep them operating efficiently. The principal government body in the nation responsible for overseeing all domestic and international airports is the Airports Authority organizations.

The National Airport Authority organisation performs the following duties:

1. Design, Development, Operation and Maintenance of international and domestic airports and civil enclaves.
2. Control and Management of the countries airspace extending beyond the territorial limits of the country, as accepted by ICAO.
3. Construction, Modification and Management of passenger terminals.
4. Development and Management of cargo terminals at international and domestic airports.
5. Provision of passenger facilities and information system at the passenger terminals at airports.
6. Expansion and strengthening of operation area, viz. Runways, Aprons, Taxiway etc.
7. Provision of visual aids.
8. Provision of Communication and Navigation aids, viz. ILS, DVOR, DME, Radar etc.

1.7 Air Traffic Zones and Approach Areas

Introduction

One of the most significant departments, air traffic control, is responsible for handling Airplanes at the airport and in the surrounding area. It provides critical information for a smooth flight departure and arrival.

A single air traffic control unit will be responsible for the control of all aircraft operating inside a specific block of airspace. Control of an aircraft or groups of aircraft, on the other hand, may be delegated to other air traffic control units as long as all air traffic control units are coordinated.

The air traffic services' objectives are to:

- Avoid collisions between aircraft;
- Avoid collisions between aircraft on the manoeuvring area and obstructions on that area;
- Expedite and maintain an orderly flow of air traffic;
- Provide advice and information useful for the safe and efficient conduct of flights.

Air Traffic Zones

The Air Traffic Zone is defined as a location where aircraft are regulated in a airport region and detailed information Is provided to aircraft pilots, ground handling agencies, and operating crews. This is accomplished using radio communications. This aids with the tracking (monitoring) of aircraft arrivals and departures, as well as the safe and efficient operation of flights.

In aviation, a controlled area is a volume of airspace that extends from the surface to a predetermined upper limit, usually around an airport, and is used to protect air traffic operating to and from that airport. Controlled airspace is defined as an area where aircraft can only fly after acquiring particular clearance from air traffic control. This implies that air traffic control at the airport knows exactly which planes are flying in that area and can take actions to ensure that they are aware of one another, such as employing separation or passing traffic information.

The Aerodrome Traffic Zone is meant to protect aerodrome traffic, i.e. traffic on the manoeuvring area and traffic in the near vicinity of an airport.

It is defined as a zone spanning from the ground up to 2000 feet with a radius of 2.5 nautical miles around the midpoint of the longest runway for aerodromes with runways longer than 1850 metres.

Approach Area

This is where planes obtain directions to get to the runway. However, Air Traffic Control (ATC) is in charge of this region, which is marked with distinct colours and symbols in accordance with the International Civil Aviation Organization's (ICAO). Because the airport is a large area, moving from one spot to another can be confusing, and we can become stranded, these sign boards assist pilots in identifying locations and moving to them according to the planned route.

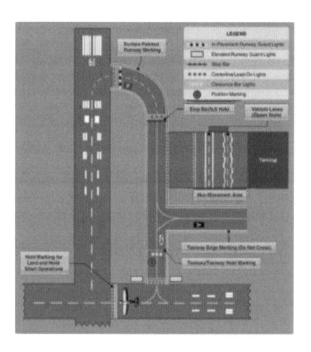

Courtesy: sl-aviation.fandom.com[/caption]

Arriving flights needed particular assistance to get to the terminal, and departing flights needed specific guidance to go to the runways. So that's everything we discovered from the sign board.

The landing approach area is marked on the runway, as are the taxiway directions. A marking symbol will be used to identify this. It is made to stand in the runways in order to prepare for take-off. Similarly, touch down markings is assigned to the landing. This aids pilots in manoeuvring

DID YOU KNOW?

Runways are designated by a number ranging from 01 to 36, which represents the magnetic azimuth of the runway's heading in decades. The local magnetic declination enables this heading to deviate from true north. A runway with the number 09 points east (90°), a runway with the number 18 points south (180°), A runway with the number 27 points west (270°), and a runway with the number 36 points north (360° rather than 0°). A plane would be heading 90 degrees when taking off or landing on runway 9. (East).

planes. The taxiway on the other side is where the planes connect to the runway in the stated directions.

1.8 Development of Airport Planning Process

Building an airport is a massive task that includes all phases from site selection to construction. It entails the design, construction, and operation of terminals, runways, and other ancillary infrastructure for airlines. Even so, it required a lot of money and is built with future growth and extension in mind. In India, the Airports Authority of India is in responsible of airport development.

Airport project design and planning are very collaborative since they entail many factors and challenges. It begins with Phases when the airports begin to operate, and as the airports grow, new phases will be implemented. Architectural & Engineering take into account design considerations. It should have a static appearance and be able to stand for long periods of time. The airport layout plans are created by architects in consultation with civil engineers. The specialists create strategic plan that are used to guide future developments.

King Khalid International Airport

Airport planning is a methodical process for developing a strategy for the efficient development of airports in accordance with local, state, and general objectives. The Airport Authority of India develops and recommends national airport layout, master, and system planning guidelines. One of the key objectives of airport planning is to guarantee that airport resources are used efficiently in order to fulfil aviation demand in a cost-effective and environmentally friendly manner.

The financial backer (Government/Private firm) can establish the airport's short- and long-term demands with effective airport planning. Airport demands may be caused by aviation demand, airport inspections, runway safety recommendations, and security recommendations.

The AAI is concerned with three approvals when planning an airport.

- **Technical Certifications**

1. Examine and accept the Airport Layout Plan (ALP).
2. Review and approval of the forecast.

3. Changes to the airspace and procedures.
4. Purchase of land.

- **Approval of Funds (Finance)**

-Once the project has received clearance for safety, security, capacity, and airport access systems, funding for the airport is granted.

- **Environmental Certifications**

1. -Examine and evaluate environmental issues.
2. -Investigate possible solutions to environmental issues.

Terminal Planning at the Airport

When planning and building a terminal, keep the following characteristics in mind:

- Peaking traffic and passenger flow.
- The shortest walking distance.
- Passenger service and sophistication levels.
- Performance benchmarks.
- Duty-free shops, restaurants, and spas are among the retail areas.
- Restrooms, ATM machines, and kiosks are all located in this area.
- Access to the shop area and service points is simple.
- Facilities that are compatible with aircraft characteristics.
- Ability to adapt to technological and automation advances.
- Future expansion capability.
- Check-in, immigration/customs clearance, baggage security screening, and baggage delivery area and processing time.

Previous chapters have discussed the components of an airport. The size of the runway and taxiway is determined by the number of flights and the needed capacity of the aircraft. Prior to the building of an airport, the aircraft apron and parking bay planning are also evaluated.

The Airport Strategy Plan ensures that the potential of available land, as well as the capacity of the runway system and terminal area, is maximized. Airports require a strong Plan to guide the rational, cost-effective, and affordable building of future infrastructure.

1.9 Costumers

Passengers are the airport's most important customers. Airport management is continuously looking for ways to improve passenger experiences. The airport serves as a hub for various businesses, most notably airlines, who operate passenger planes.

The airport authority is in constant contact with members of the community, such as chambers of commerce, the local tourism board, passengers, and business people. They discussed their desires and received comments to create a list of top goals for the guests.

Business or leisure, scheduled or charter, originating or destined, and transfer or transit are all common classifications for passengers. Business travellers typically pay much higher tickets, and airlines typically want to attract such traffic by providing a high level of service.

Passenger's choice factor

- Passengers choose air travel to save time over other modes of transportation. In terms of check-in and boarding, the airport has provided excellent service.
- Flight frequency Some passengers choose to fly out of airports that provide them more choice in terms of departure and arrival times, as well as numerous flight frequencies.
- Airport Connectivity: The majority of travellers prefer modes of transportation that can swiftly connect them to the airport, such as train, metro, or shuttle buses.
- Air costs are proven to have a direct impact on whether travellers pick between flight options. When all other factors are equal, passengers prefer to fly from an airport where they can get a lower airfare for their journey.

1.10 Airline Decision and Other Airport Operations

Airline Decision

Airliners are the primary occupants of airports, and airport design must meet all of their requirements in accordance with international standards. The airline determines what type of aircraft service it will provide to the airport. Airlines pay the airport based on how much space they use. Airport fees are divided into categories such as aircraft landing fees, parking fees, and apron facility fees, and ground handling services are determined by the airline, which can either deploy their own staff or hire third-party services to provide ground handling services.

Airlines, as the principal occupants of airport terminal buildings, have highly specific needs for space and facilities within the terminal area. It is consequently critical to seek and keep their input, cooperation, and participation in the review process throughout the design period. In addition, the airline facilities planner may provide vital information on passenger and aircraft type forecasts, as well as technical expertise on many elements of airport architecture. For this information and support, contact the headquarters of any airline that serves a specific airport directly.

Airport Operations

The operation of an airport in the aviation industry can be a difficult task. An airport is much more than a collection of planes that take off and land on a runway. It's a lot more complicated than that. It usually comprises of a large runway that is mostly used for commercial flights. In addition to parking and maintenance facilities, most airports have a control tower.

Larger airports may have multiple terminals, aprons, taxiway bridges, airport security centres, and passenger facilities such as restaurants and lounges. A significant number of autos will be driving about the airfield in addition to those in the air. Keeping everything in order and in sync is a difficult task. Furthermore, aviation operations are complex since they involve a system of aircraft support, passenger services, and aircraft control.

Four types of airport operations are commonly used. The areas of ground operations, airside operations, billing and invoicing, and information management must all be handled. They must all work together to guarantee that everything runs smoothly and properly, as previously indicated.

- **Ground operations**: Ensure the safety of passengers and a pleasant customer experience at the airport. Maintaining a clean environment in the halls. Maintaining the airport's roads in proper working order. Keeping an eye on the properties in the close surroundings of the airport.

- **Airside operations**: Responding to mishaps, accidents, and emergencies on the airfield. Allocation of aircraft parking and escorts. Runways and taxiways should be inspected on a regular basis. Wildlife management on a day-to-day basis to lessen the risk of bird strikes on aircraft.

- **Billing** and invoicing is an element of airport operations that is rarely visible to the general public, yet it is vital to keeping planes flying. It is in charge of both aeronautical and non-aeronautical revenue. Advanced accounting systems are often in place to manage flight bills, invoicing, cash, and sales within the airport, as well as other aspects of airport finance, such as point-of-sale and employee payrolls.

- **Information management**: As passengers or airlines, we require reliable and up-to-date information from the airport and its users. Typical information management responsibilities include recording seasonal and arrival/departure information as well as maintaining track of airline connections.

Airport operations is further divided into different divisions that assist the

DID YOU KNOW?

Changi International has been rated the greatest airport in the world for the past seven years by Skytrax as of 2021. It's not hard to see why. Not only does it work well and provide exquisite amenities, but it also provides a spectacular and unforgettable experience for people travelling by.

airport in generating cash, such as renting out stores and space for commercial use. These services are provided by a third party.

Furthermore, the airport continues to develop and inoculate available places in order to provide passengers and airlines with a hassle-free and superior experience.

CHAPTER 2

PLANNING AND DESIGNING THE TERMINAL AREA

29

The design phase of an airport is dependent on the future forecast of airport operations, as we learned in the previous chapter. It all starts with the runways, apron, terminal, and passenger vehicle parking area, which is one of the airport's primary categories.

2.1 Operational Concept

The design phase of an airport is dependent on the future forecast of airport operations, as we learned in the previous chapter. It all starts with the runways, apron, terminal, and passenger vehicle parking area, which is one of the airport's primary categories.

The performance of the future air transportation system is described in five categories in the Integrated Plan's consideration of operational concepts:

- Operations of security
- Assurance of safety
- Airport Operations
- Aircraft Operations
- ATM operation

When safety and security are seen as inherent in each operational step, when they are integrated into each phase from the start, and when they are regarded an integral component of system reliability and efficiency, the best results are attained. When safety and security are patched onto technologies and processes by an outside party after the process of establishing operational technologies and processes has already begun, they are less effective.

Furthermore, just as safety can be improved by employing numerous, redundant systems, security can be improved by employing a layered system in which several security features are linked and provide backup.

Layered security, on the other hand, is only effective if it is directed by a risk-based approach that quantifies the cost of each layer as well as its contribution to overall security risk reduction goals.

The Integrated Plan's other three performance areas—airports, airplanes, and ATM—reflect how responsibility for the manufacture, ownership, and operation of physical assets are split among different groups, but they do not correlate to separate operational stages.

Bangalore Airport Terminal Waiting Area

Operation concept it must be able to comprehend both future and current planning requirements, such as increasing passenger capacity and the number of flights available in the future. The airport planning team provides the required documentation to the appropriate authority for approval of the airport building project. In this unit, we will learn how the terminal is constructed and what components play a role in this process.

The process of designing airport passenger terminal facilities must include a wide range of safety, operational, commercial, financial, and environmental factors, as well as local government and airline sector interests and goals. A thorough overview of these interrelated factors can be found in Planning Considerations.

Building a new airport terminal building or expanding an existing one necessitates extensive coordination and involvement from a variety of airport users and other interested parties. It is as a result. It is critical that the architect-engineer establish and maintain a line of contact with all of these groups from the start. Until the finish of the project The needs and suggestions of Each group will be distinct and, in some situations, at odds with one another. Other than that, or with the overall design concept. These disagreements must be reconciled. Prior to the design stage, negotiate and/or compromise. To prevent missing vital details. It results in costly and time-consuming design adjustments as a result of user requirements. It's usually a good idea to form a facilities development advisory council for the terminal construction project.

Airport management representatives, airline facilities planning representatives, chosen building tenants and concessionaires, and other airport users and parties with a particular interest in the facility should make up this advisory council. This committee is usually chaired by the airport manager or a representative of the airport owner.

Bangalore Airport Terminal Waiting Area

2.2 Space Relationships and Area Requirement

The area requirement relationships are separated into two categories. The first is for aircraft operations, and the second is for passenger services. It is critical to keep track of how much space is available for each service. Let's take a closer look at each of these areas.

2.3 The relationship between the terminal and the airfield

The following factors influence the terminal building's relative location in relation to the airfield.

A. Considerations for Aircraft the position of the passenger terminal on the airport is affected by the taxiing and parking of air carrier aircraft, as well as the size and type of aircraft. Consider the following factors:

- **Circulation of aircraft.** From the passenger terminal to the ends of the primary runway, aircraft taxiing routes for takeoff should be as direct as possible. Landing aircraft should evacuate runways as rapidly as possible into taxiways in order to reduce taxiing lengths to the terminal and free up runway space for other planes. As a result, it is preferable to site the passenger terminal centrally in relation to the principal runways, avoiding the need for landing or leaving aircraft to cross active runways when taxiing to and from the parking apron, if at all possible. This will cut down on expensive and time-consuming aircraft taxiing while also saving fuel.

- **Parking of aircraft**. The passenger terminal is close to an aircraft parking apron. At the aircraft parking apron, people, baggage, freight, and mail are loaded and unloaded, as well as aircraft fueling, service, and light maintenance. The depth of the apron required for aircraft manoeuvring and parking determines the distance between the passenger terminal and adjacent runways and taxiways.

- **Types of Aircraft.** Domestic air carriers currently operate a wide range of aircraft. The size, weight, and passenger capacity of these planes varies greatly. The runway and taxiway separations, as well as building and obstacle clearances and setback requirements, are governed by the kind of aircraft in use and predicted in the future. The area of the ramp required for aircraft parking and manoeuvring is determined by the size of the aircraft, and the aircraft capacity affects the sizing of passenger handling and amenities within the terminal building.

2.4 Terminal's relationship to other airport facilities

The main fixed elements of a passenger terminal complex addressed in this chapter should be located-to allow for future growth of each without encroaching on the passenger terminal or adjacent facilities.

- **Air Carrier Control and Terminal Navigation Facilities** : All approach areas, runways, and taxiways must be visible to the airport traffic control tower without obstruction. If the control tower is far away from the passenger terminal, the terminal building and its outbuildings must be positioned and kept to a minimum height so that sight lines from the tower to these vital parts of the airport are not obstructed.

- **Other Activities in Airport**: The terminal construction location should be in an area of the airport that is large enough to support current and future roadway networks and parking facilities, as well as other airport activities that might benefit from proximity to the passenger terminal. Other areas of the airport, such as Air Cargo Facilities, Aircraft Refuelling Facilities, Rental Car Storage and Maintenance, and Crash/Fire/Rescue, are also essential. The airport is prioritized in terms of the importance of the area for vital airport services.

2.5 Area Requirement

Any airport must choose a landing zone. According to the airport administration, a variety of things must be considered prior to development.

The following are site criteria that may impact the terminal area's location:

a. The environment. Topographical conditions can play a big role in deciding where to place the passenger terminal. Although it is normally more cost effective to use reasonably level land with good drainage, an existing topography feature such as a grade differential between the landside of the terminal and the aeroplane ramp can often be included into the terminal concept.

b. Existing Conditions: Existing infrastructure and utilities must be preserved. Inventoried and taken into account in the planning of new or expanded facilities terminals for passengers.

c. Potential for Expansion: Potential expansion beyond predicted requirements should always be considered in order to ensure the long-term success of a new passenger terminal or an addition to an existing terminal.

d. Impacts on the Environment: A terminal building facility's location, or a big extension of an existing one, could have severe environmental consequences.

e. Connection to the Highway System: Air travellers, staff, greeters, guests, truckers, and ground transportation businesses all require access to the airport terminal area. The private automobile remains the primary form of transportation to smaller airports with easy access for passengers and personnel.

2.6 Noise Control

The airplane jet sound is one of the first things we notice as we approach the airport. It's important to keep these things in mind because airplanes have large engines that need to be run and tested before they can be dispatched. However, sound would be an issue for other people such as passengers, airport employees, and residents living near an airport. This can be remedied using the engineering methodology, which eliminates sound noise.

Sound from aircraft engines is carried into the terminal building and becomes a concern when it causes pain or interferes with communication. The frequency of the noise and the length of exposure to it have an impact on tolerance. Medium-to-high-frequency noise, such as that produced by jet aircraft, will disturb speech and hearing more than a low-frequency tone of same intensity. Noise difficulties are most common when the jet engines are turned on and when taxiing out from the terminal. While it is not practicable to prepare for expensive noise control measures, terminal construction should be robust and made of dense materials, with first-rate workmanship to avoid the majority of issues.

Construction materials should be of a sort that allows for future additions or adjustments to be made without difficulty. The allowable noise level for each of the specialized terminal building regions varies according on the area's function. If positioned on the field side of the building, operational and baggage-handling facilities with higher levels of noise tolerance will operate as a noise barrier for more sensitive terminal spaces. Wherever practical, the room's shortest wall should face the source of noise. The use of thick building materials and the integration of spaces within walls minimize noise transmission.

2.7 Vehicular Traffic and Parking at Airports

Roadway System Managing Vehicular Traffic:

The roadway system must be considered concurrently with the planning of the terminal building and auto and aircraft parking. Connection to Highway Network. Access to the airport terminal area is required by air travellers, employees, greeters, visitors, truckers, and ground transportation companies. The private automobile continues to be the major mode of transportation to smaller airports and, as a result, air travellers and terminal area employees will be the main contributors to terminal area traffic. The passenger terminal should, therefore, when possible, be located on the side of the airport nearest to the population centre generating the major source of traffic to the airport or the highway serving it.

The location of the terminal with respect to the highway should allow sufficient distance to accommodate present and future vehicular traffic concepts such as diamond intersections and the ultimate terminal area development. Inadequate space for proper roadway alignment and possible interchanges is one of the most inhibiting factors of future terminal development.

Airport Parking Space

2.8 Parking at Airport:

Public parking facilities should be provided for in proximity to the passenger's terminal for the airline passengers, visitors, and other terminal users, while parking requirements and characteristics vary from airport to airport. Another key source of revenue for airport management is parking fees. Due to the fact that these are provided with airport accessibility. There are various forms of parking. Let's take a closer look at each one individually.

- **Terminal curb** : An airport's terminal curb front is a complicated working environment. Many different kinds of automobiles approach and halt at the curb. Private autos, taxis, limousines, parking lot buses, rental car buses, regional buses, and hotel shuttles and shuttle buses are among these modes of transportation. These areas are used for passenger drop-offs and pick-ups. At this time, the airport does not charge for parking. However, there will be a time limit for the stop. During peak hours, just a few spaces are reserved exclusively.

- **Short & Long term parking**- When you'll be gone for less than a week and need to park your car at the airport; short-term airport parking is the best option. This is also where you can park if you're picking up or dropping off someone at the airport. When comparing the cost per day, short-term airport parking is more expensive than long-term airport parking. If you plan to leave your car at the airport overnight, you may end up paying more than the daily rate for long-term parking.

Some airports provide long-term parking depending on the facilities available. When you need to be out of town for a week or more, long-term airport parking is the way to go. You'll also need a parking lot to park your automobile properly. Short-term airport parking is substantially more expensive than long-term airport parking.

- **Employee Vehicle Parking:** Terminal employees should be able to park within walking distance of the terminal. The number of terminal area staff parking spots necessary is usually determined by communicating with airport management, terminal tenants, or providing 10% to 20% of expected public parking space requirements.
- **Rental Car Parking**: A minimum of 10 parking spaces for each rental business with a terminal counter must be supplied in close proximity to the terminal building, usually near the baggage claim area, at low-traffic airports. The amount of space to supply is governed by the local government's requirements. Rental car wash, service, and storage facilities are usually found outside of the terminal complex.

Parking sign: Parking Lot Entrances and Exits To avoid any confusion, parking lot entry and departure locations should be clearly marked and well-spaced. A single exit is preferred when fees are charged. The exit should be located such that the parking customer may pick up passengers and luggage at the terminal curb.

CHAPTER 3

AIR TRAFFIC CONTROL AND NAVIGATION AIDS

3.1 Air Traffic Control and Aids

Flying an airplane is challenging since it requires not only balancing the plane but also maintaining proper height and navigation In order to provide enough information to the aircraft, many departments were involved in this work. Another department is Air Traffic Control, which is in charge of coordinating all aircraft in specific zones and supporting them in flying efficiently and properly.

Air traffic control: It's a service provided by ground-based air traffic controllers who guide planes on the ground and through controlled airspace, as well as providing advice to planes flying in uncontrolled airspace.

The primary purpose of air traffic control (ATC) around the world is to prevent crashes, organize and expedite air traffic flow, and provide pilots with information and other assistance. In certain nations, ATC is used for security or defence, or it is managed by the military.

Air traffic controllers use radar to track flights in their designated region, while pilots converse via radio. ATC maintains traffic separation requirements to prevent crashes by ensuring that each aircraft has a minimum amount of empty space around it at all times. ATC's services are available to any private, military, and commercial aircraft flying inside the airspace of a number of countries. ATC may issue orders that pilots must obey or advisories (known as flight information in some countries) that pilots may disregard at their discretion, depending on the kind of flight and the class of airspace. The pilot in command has final control over the aircraft's safe operation in an emergency and may diverge from ATC orders. Stray from ATC directives to the extent necessary to keep their aircraft safe to fly.

The following represent a few examples of air traffic control aids:

· It provides the necessary effective positive assistance for air navigation. Control aids are grouped into a variety of techniques and methods.

· It offers effective communication to ground staff, known as external help, and within the cockpit, known as internal aids.

· Air traffic control aids are categorized into two categories for improved performance and ease. Airways aids or en route aids.

3.2 Runways and Taxiways Markings

The information provided by airport pavement markings and signs is useful to pilots during take-off, landing, and taxiing. Airport markings and signs that are consistent from one airport to the next promote safety and efficiency. Pilots are encouraged to collaborate with airport operators to meet the marking and sign standards outlined in this section. The runway markings are white. Yellow markings indicate taxiways.

Airport Pavement Markings: The airport pavement markings have been divided into four categories for the purpose of this section:

    a) Runway Markings.
    b) Taxiway Markings.
    c) Holding Position Markings.
    d) Other Markings.

  a) **Runway Marking**

Runway marking is essential because it directs pilots to landing aircraft. It is one of the most important elements for marking signs. It's usually done in accordance with ICAO or AAI guidelines. The runway is designed for take-off and landing. It is marked with a centre - line and strips so that the pilot can estimate the aircraft's position relative to the runway.

- The runway numbers and letters are determined by the approach orientation. The runway number is the full number closest to one tenth of the runway centreline's magnetic azimuth, measured clockwise from magnetic north. Depending on the situation, the letters distinguish between parallel runways on the left (L), right (R), or centre (C):

1. For two parallel runways "L" "R."
2. For three parallel runways "L" "C" "R."

- Marking the centreline of the runway. The runway centreline marks the runway's centre and serves as a guide for take-off and landing alignment.
- Aiming Points on the Runway A landing aircraft's visual aiming point is the aiming point marking. A broad white stripe is situated on each side of the runway centreline, roughly 1,000 feet from the landing threshold, in these two rectangular marks.
- Touchdown Zone Markers on the Runway The touchdown zone markings define the landing zone and are coded to provide distance information in 500-foot (150-meter) increments. These markers are made up of symmetrically aligned pairs of one, two, and three rectangular bars around the runway centreline.
- Threshold Markings on the Runway There are two types of runway threshold markings. They are made up of eight uniformly sized longitudinal stripes arranged symmetrically along the runway centreline. A threshold marking aids in identifying the start of the runway that is open for landing. The landing threshold may be shifted or displaced in various cases.

b) Taxiway Marking:

A taxiway is a route that connects runways to aprons, hangars, terminals, and other airport buildings. They are generally made of hard surfaces like asphalt or concrete, though smaller general aviation airports may include gravel or grass as well.

Whenever a taxiway crosses a runway, it should be marked with a centreline and a runway holding position. Taxiway edge markers are used to distinguish the taxiway from other pavement that is not intended for aircraft use or to demarcate the taxiway's edge.

The majority of airports do not have a defined taxiing speed limit (though some do). Based on barriers, there is a basic rule for safe speed. There may be limitations imposed by operators and aircraft manufacturers. 20-30 knots (37-56 km/h; 23-35 mph) is a typical cab speed.

c) Holding Position Marking

Runway Holding Position Markings serve as a critical guideline for aircraft operations. They define the precise location where aircraft are required to come to a complete stop when approaching a runway. Comprising four distinct yellow lines, consisting of two solid lines and two dashed lines, these markings are spaced either six or twelve inches apart and extend across the full width of the taxiway or runway.

These markings play a crucial role at specific airports, particularly those where it's imperative to ensure that an aircraft remains stationary on a taxiway situated within the vicinity of a runway's approach or departure path. This is essential to prevent any potential interference with the ongoing activities on that particular runway.

Essentially, the runway holding position markings function as a clear signal to pilots, indicating the precise point at which they must halt and wait before entering an area that could potentially disrupt the safe approach of aircraft preparing to land. You will typically encounter these markings on taxiways located near the approach zones where aircraft are descending for their final landing.

d) Other Marking

Additional markings can often be observed on runways and taxiways, primarily along the edges, to provide essential guidance to pilots regarding turning points, distances, and specific entry details for airport areas.

These markings typically consist of two solid yellow lines running parallel to the taxiway centreline, clearly defining the boundary of the taxiway. They serve the crucial purpose of assisting pilots in maintaining their aircraft within the designated taxiing area, ensuring safe and efficient ground operations.

In addition to these markings, there are also a variety of signage installations strategically placed throughout the airport. These signs serve as valuable navigational aids by displaying taxiway and runway identifiers, directional information, and other critical data, all of which play a vital role in guiding both pilots and air traffic controllers during ground operations. These navigational aids are indispensable for ensuring precise and safe maneuvering on the airport's surface.

3.3 Day & Night Landing Aids

We will focus on Day & Night Landing Aids in this chapter. We won't get too deeply into the technical aspects, but we will understand how to employ the instruments that are used for aircraft landing both during the day and at night.

The critical phase of an aircraft's journey is its landing; hence it is essential that it is pointed in the appropriate direction to ensure a successful landing. We shall first understand daytime and landing. based on the technical terminology

Day Landing Aids

In aviation, visual flight rules (VFR) are a set of rules that a pilot must observe when flying an aircraft in weather that is clear enough for the pilot to see where the aircraft is heading. In particular, the weather has to be better than the minimal requirements for basic VFR flight, or in visual meteorological conditions (VMC), as described in the regulations of the responsible aviation authority.

The pilot must be able to control the aircraft while keeping an eye on the ground and keeping a visual distance from obstacles and other aircraft. Pilots must utilise instrument flight rules and operate the aircraft primarily by using the instruments rather than visual reference if the weather is less than VMC. A VFR flight may request permission from air traffic control to operate as Special VFR in a control zone.

Night Landing Aids

When there is little visual reference to the ground, pilots use the instrument aids. Here, the instruments receive various data about the flight location from ground-based radar and satellite transmission that is displayed in the cockpit. Additionally, the pilot receives associated data for flight plans and can then make the necessary decisions, such as adjusting direction or altitude, as needed.

But there must be some illumination setups for the pilots to use when bringing an aircraft down in an airport. Any flashing light, radio beacon, communication device, radar device, or system of similar devices can serve as a landing aid to assist an aircraft during approach and landing.

used to direct a pilot to the runway, aids in determining the pilot's alignment with the runway and the proper angle of approach.

Various landing aids

- Instruments landing system (ILS)
- Precision approach radar (PAR) or ground approach control (GAC)
- Airport surveillance radar (ASR)
- Airport surface detection equipment (ASDE)
- Approach lights

3.4 Airport Lighting and Other Associated Aids

Lighting aids play a significant role in airports at night, particularly in helping aircraft pilots understand the location of the airport and other required parameters. As the marking sign becomes more obvious as we get closer, it becomes more difficult to understand the location if we are far away; in these circumstances, lighting can assist. Furthermore, the light linked with the runway is important for aircraft, which has a significant use that we shall study in this section, and the taxiway assists aircraft in guiding them to a specific location at the airport.

Approach lighting systems, which consist of a series of high-intensity white lights that run along the runway's centreline and extend up to 600 metres (2,000 feet) beyond the threshold, also provide visual guidance to approaching aircraft. Landing-zone lighting is provided over the first 900 metres (3,000 feet) from the runway threshold at airfields where visibility is poor. These lights, which are installed in patterns flush with the runway pavement, give guidance until touchdown.

A variety of guidance light systems help to clearly define the runway. A line of green lights marks the threshold, while white lights flash toward the moving aircraft at regular intervals to mark the margins and centreline. A line of red lights at the end of the usable pavement alerts the pilot of the approaching runway end. Blue boundary lights and green centreline lights occur at regular intervals to distinguish taxiways.

Let's understand about the runway lights.

When an aircraft approaches the runway, the runway light guides the aircraft to its exact position. On the other hand, the runway light indicates the pilot's location relative to the runway and assists him in setting the approaching directions.

A. Runway Lights

We will discuss various types of runway lights during the session.

- **Approach Light Systems (ALS)**

The basic means of transitioning from instrument flight to visual flight for landing are provided by ALS. The sophistication and configuration of an approach light system for a specific runway are determined by operational requirements.

- **Visual Glideslope Indicators**

There are five types of visual glideslope indicators that help pilots land aircraft based on lighting indications. These indicators help pilots align their aircraft to the centre line of the runway and control their speed so they can land in the correct position. This will be useful due to the runway's low visibility and bad weather conditions.

To help pilots verify they are flying the correct approach angle to the runway, visual approach slope indicators use a combination of white and red lights next to the runway.

- **Visual Approach Slope Indicator (VASI)**

The individual lightboxes that make a VASI work are made of two light bulbs with a solid partition between them. The red light is below the white light. The box is positioned on the ground at the desired angle for the light to shift.

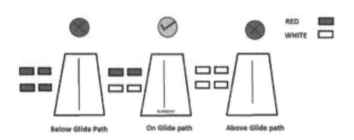

Below Glide Path   On Glide path   Above Glide path

- **Precision Approach Path Indicator (PAPI)** : Light units similar to the VASI are used in the precision approach path indicator (PAPI), but they are arranged in a single row of two or four light units. These lights can be seen from up to 20 miles away at night and up to 5 miles away during the day. Within 10 degrees of the extended runway centreline and up to 3.4 nautical miles from the runway threshold, the PAPI's visual glide path typically provides safe obstruction clearance. Until the aircraft is visually aligned with the runway.

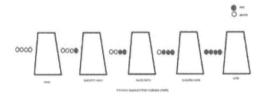

- **Tri-colour Systems**

In most tri-color visual approach slope indicators, a single light unit projects a three-color visual approach path into the final approach area of the runway where the indicator is positioned. The below glide path indicator is red, the above glide path indicator is amber, and the on glide path indicator is green.

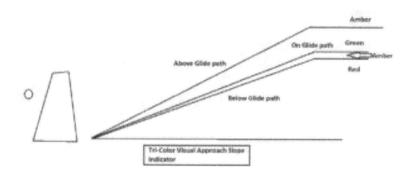

1. **Runway End Identifier Lights**

REILs are used at several airports to provide quick and accurate identification of a runway's approach end. The system consists of a pair of synchronized flashing lights located laterally on either side of the runway threshold. The approach area REILs can be either omnidirectional or unidirectional.

2. **Runway Edge Light Systems**

During moments of darkness or limited visibility, runway edge lights are used to delineate the boundaries of runways. These light systems are categorized based on the amount of intensity or brightness they can provide.

3. **Runway Centreline Lighting System (RCLS)**

Some precision approach runways have runway centreline lights added to help with landing in low visibility situations. They run the length of the runway and are spaced at 50-foot intervals.

4. **Lights in the Touchdown Zone (TDZL).**

Some precision approach runways have touchdown zone lights installed to identify the touchdown zone while landing in low visibility conditions. They are made up of two rows of transverse light bars symmetrically arranged around the runway centreline.

5. **Runway Status Light (RWSL) System**

RWSL is a completely automated system that gives pilots and surface vehicle operators with runway status information, clearly indicating when it is unsafe to enter, traverse, take off from, or land on a runway. In line with the position and velocity of detected surface traffic and approach traffic, the RWSL system analyses information from surveillance systems and activates Runway Entrance Lights (REL) and Take off Hold Lights (THL).

B. Taxiway Lights

- **Taxiway Edge Lights:** Lights along the edge of the taxiway. During periods of darkness or limited visibility, taxiway edge lights are used to indicate the borders of taxiways. Blue light is emitted by these fixtures.
- **Taxiway Centreline Lights:** Centreline Lights on the Taxiway In low-visibility situations, taxiway centreline lights are utilized to help ground traffic. On straight segments of the taxiway, they are situated along the centreline in a straight line, on the centreline of curved portions, and along authorized taxiing pathways in portions of runways, ramps, and apron areas.
- **Clearance Bar Lights :** Bar Lights with a Clearance In low visibility situations, clearance bar lights are installed at holding positions on taxiways to increase the visibility of the holding position. They can also be utilized at night to locate an intersecting taxiway.
- **Runway Guard Lights :** At taxiway/runway crossings, runway guard lights are erected. They're mostly utilized to make taxiway/runway intersections more visible in low-visibility situations, but they can be employed in all weather.

C. Aeronautical light beacon.

Colour light will be utilized to signify the type of place, such as an airport, a heliport, a landmark, a specific point on a Federal airway in hilly terrain, or an obstruction, in order to identify the location quickly. A rotating beacon or one or more flashing lights could be employed. A visual NAVAID flashing flashes of white and/or coloured light is known as an aeronautical light beacon.

D. Obstruction Lights

During daytime and night time situations, obstructions are marked/lighted to alert airmen to their presence. They can be marked or lit in any of the following   ways:
Red Obstruction Lights for Aviation. During night time operations, flashing aviation red beacons (20 to 40 flashes per minute) and steady burning aviation red lights are used. Daytime marking is done with aviation orange and white paint.

CHAPTER 4

AIRPORT PLANNING AND SURVEYS

Airport planning is the process of developing guidelines for the effective development of airports in accordance with local, state, and national goals. One of the most essential objectives of airport planning is to guarantee that airport resources are used efficiently in order to fulfil aviation demand in a cost-effective manner. Airport planning can be as broad as a national system plan or as specific as a single airport master plan.

4.1 Airport Planning and Surveys

Airport planning is the process of developing guidelines for the effective development of airports in accordance with local, state, and national goals. One of the most essential objectives of airport planning is to guarantee that airport resources are used efficiently in order to fulfil aviation demand in a cost-effective manner. Airport planning can be as broad as a national system plan or as specific as a single airport master plan.

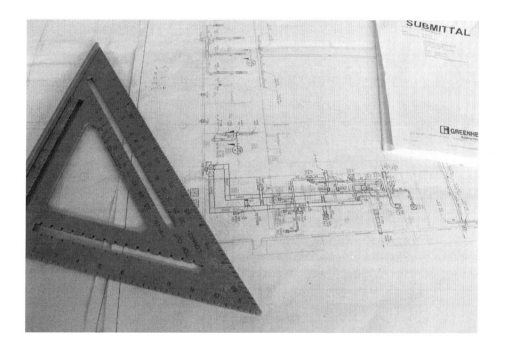

An airport master plan is a long-term expansion strategy for the airport. The following are some of the goals of a master plan:

- Forecasting the future requirement of airport for in terms of the passengers and cargo operations. so we need identify the space requirements for operations.
- In a graphic manner, represent existing airport characteristics, projected airport growth, and predicted land usage.
- To establish a realistic schedule for the completion of the projected development.
- To devise a workable financial plan to fund the development.
- Validate the plan on a technical and procedural level by looking into concepts and alternatives from a technical, economic, and environmental standpoint.

- By drafting and presenting a plan to the public that successfully addresses all major concerns and meets with local, state, and federal criteria, a foundation for a continuous planning process will be established.

The intent of To start up the plan develop an airport its really important to understand the site suitability for the constructions since we required to survey the engineering requirements and as well suitability of Aeronautical operational. That's also should be support the future plan of the airport.

In India all the site approval has to get it done by the Airport Authority of India which the pre-select for the locations. Further they get involve to take further steps to bring to the plans.

Site Selection Report Requirements

Airport is the key factor most of the important transportation for business and it is also seeks good amount of the capital. so considering the for construction airport we should go through lot of factors, in that one first site selection. In site selection it is consider understand is it suitable for airport construction by understanding with Soil test , Local objections ,

Airport Survey

The airport project necessitates extensive inquiry and critical assessment from a variety of perspectives. The preliminary survey data and details are thoroughly analysed, and the detailed survey results are included in the recommendation report for the proposed airport site. This chapter provides a quick overview of the typical thorough surveys conducted to determine the viability of an airport location.

Survey Objective: The following are the primary goals or aims for conducting detailed surveys:

- To determine soil properties.
- To gather information necessary for the design of various airport components.
- Demarcate the ground on a blueprint and begin the land purchase proceedings.
- To provide an understanding of the weather conditions at the suggested site.
- To make provisions for future airport expansion.
- To create appropriate drawings.
- To submit a report for approval by the appropriate responsible authority.
- To propose measures, if any, to improve the current site conditions.

4.2 Runway Length and Width, Sight Distances

A runway is technically defined as "a rectangular area on a land aerodrome prepared for aircraft landing and takeoff." Runways can be man-made (often asphalt, concrete, or a combination of the two) or natural (grass, dirt, gravel, ice, sand, or salt). Runways, as well as taxiways and ramps, are sometimes referred to as "tarmac," though tarmac is used on very few runways.

Because aircraft roll at high speeds, a runway is essential for smooth landings and takeoffs. It should be built in accordance with international standards.

Runway dimensions range from 245 m (804 ft) long and 8 m (26 ft) wide in smaller general aviation airports to 5,500 m (18,045 ft) long and 80 m (262 ft) wide in larger general international airports.

It should meet the following basic requirements:

- Take-off Run Available – The length of runway declared available and suitable for an airplane's ground run before take-off.
- Take-off Distance Available – The length of the available take-off run plus the length of the clearway, if one is provided.
- Accelerate-Stop Distance Available – The length of the available take-off run plus the length of the stop way, if one is provided.
- Landing Distance Available – The length of runway declared available and suitable for an airplane's ground run.

Runway Width

- Depends on the type of airport and the largest aircraft in operation
- In the case of a large aircraft, the central 30 metre width of the runway pavement is observed to take more concentrated air-traffic load
- It also requires additional space on the two sides of this 30 metre width, in order to protect the farthest machinery that is engines, from ingestion of loos.

Sight Distance:

For individual runways, the ICAO sight distance requirement requires that the runway profile allow an unobstructed view between any two points at a specified height above the runway centre line to be mutually visible for at least one-half the runway length. According to ICAO, these two points must be 1.5 metres (5 feet) above the runway for aerodrome code letter A runways, 2 metres (7 feet) above the runway for aerodrome code letter B runways, and 3 metres (10 feet) above the runway for aerodrome code letter C, D, or E runways.

4.3 Longitudinal and Transverse

Runways are constructed using a variety of materials to withstand aircraft weight and landing pressure. They are also able to withstand extremely high or low temperatures. However, some elements of the runway still need to be covered to ensure a proper water drainage system without compromising the runway's flatness.

The few components that helped aircraft land and take off made up the remainder of the runway. We will learn about the transverse and longitudinal grade restrictions of the runway in this chapter. These are the areas where some of the surface angles are being adjusted.

The slopes of the runway surface are determined by the aircraft approach types. Standards are divided into two categories: A and B and C, D, and E. The runway pavement, shoulders, and areas near to the runway are all subject to longitudinal and transverse limits. Smooth transitions between pavement surfaces that cross each other are ideal. Depending on whatever category it falls under, the dominant runway takes precedence when two runways overlap.

In a connection between a runway and a taxiway, the runway is given precedence. Future runway expansions or enhancements should be accounted for in design grades to suit increasingly stringent aircraft approach categories. Minimum transverse gradients that satisfy drainage needs should be used. Despite the fact that there is a provision for alternate runways or taxiways inside the

Transverse slope

Except in cases where a single cross fall from high to low in the direction of the wind most usually associated with rain would ensure rapid drainage, the runway surface must be cambered to encourage the most rapid drainage of water. Transverse slope requirements are:

If the code letter is C, D, E, or F, the rate is 1.5%; if it's A or B, the rate is 2%.

However, in any case, the slope must not be less than 1% or greater than 2%, depending on the situation, with the exception of runway or taxiway crossings where gentler slopes may be required. The transverse slope for a cambered surface must be symmetrical on both sides of the centre line. Except for where a runway intersects with another runway or a taxiway, where an even transition must be provided while taking into account the necessity for proper drainage, the transverse slope must be essentially constant along the length of a runway.

Longitudinal slopes

When the code number is 3 or 4, and 1 or 2, the slope calculated by dividing the difference between the greatest and minimum elevation along the runway center line by the length of the runway is not to be greater than: — 1%; and — 2%. No part of a runway may have a longitudinal slope that is greater than: 1.25 percent where the code number is 4, with the exception of the beginning and last quarters of the runway, where the longitudinal slope may not be greater than 0.8 percent;

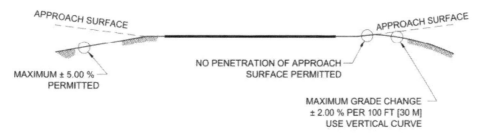

LONGITUDINAL GRADE

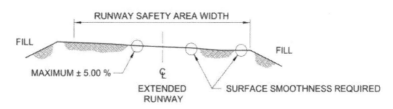

NOTE: TRANSITIONS BETWEEN DIFFERENT GRADIENTS SHOULD BE WARPED SMOOTHLY.

TRANSVERSE GRADE

4.4 Runway Intersections, Taxiways, Clearances, Aprons, Holding Apron. Numbering

Runway Intersections:

Two or more runways that intersect or intersect within their lengths, when there are moderately high winds from more than one direction during the year, an intersecting runway arrangement is used. Only one runway is generally used in high wind conditions. In light wind conditions, however, both runways may be operated concurrently. Typically, the runway that is in operation for the majority of the year is designated as the instrument runway.

Many airports have overlapping runways, mostly for expansion purposes, but also to provide a minimal crosswind option when wind direction varies. While using both runways concurrently may increase aircraft efficiency by allowing shorter approach tracks and taxi routes, there are significant inherent risks associated with concurrent operation of intersecting runways; strict regulations must be in place to prevent a runway incursion.

In terms of total throughput, using just one runway in mixed mode typically provides the same capacity as using both runways, but with a substantially lower likelihood of runway incursion difficulties.

Operations

These runway operations are carried out by ATC, who decide which runway to maintain operating and provide further updates to aircraft pilots. Such operations are hard since there are many runways and connecting taxiways, but they are highly valued in terms of safety and standards.

Taxiways that connect to the runway must likewise hold position before joining the runway; only after clearance may it proceed to the runway.

Taxiway Markings

Every taxiway that intersects a runway should include centreline markers and runway holding position markings. Taxiway edge markers are used to divide the taxiway from pavement that is not intended for aircraft use or to designate the taxiway's border.

A taxiway is an airport path that connects runways, aprons, hangars, terminals, and other buildings. They typically have a firm surface like asphalt or concrete, while smaller general aviation airports may have gravel or grass.

Most airports do not have a set taxi speed limit (though some do). Based on the barriers, there is a basic rule for safe speed. Operators and aircraft manufacturers may have constraints. Taxi speeds are often in the 20-30 knot range (37-56 km/h; 23-35 mph).

Marking:

- Typical Centreline A single continuous yellow line ranging in width from 15 centimetres (6 in) to 30 centimetres (12 in).
- Improved Centreline A parallel line of yellow dashes on either side of the taxiway centreline is the enhanced taxiway centre line marker. Before a runway holding position marking, taxiway centrelines are strengthened for 150 feet (46 m).
- Dashed markings designate the margin of a taxiway on a paved surface where the surrounding pavement, such as an apron, is designed for aircraft use. These markers are made up of a broken double yellow line that is at least 15 centimetres (6 in) wide.
- Markings for Geographic Location These markers are placed at strategic spots along low visibility taxi paths (when the visual range of the runway is less than 1200 feet (370 m). They are located to the left of the taxiway centerline in the taxiing direction.
- Markings for Runway Holding Positions These indicate where an aeroplane should come to a halt when approaching a runway from a

taxiway. They are made up of four yellow lines, two solid and two dashed, spaced six or twelve inches (15 or 30 cm) apart and running the length of the taxiway or runway.

4.5 ATC Runway Clearance

ATC clearances are provided based on known traffic and physical airport circumstances. An ATC clearance is an authority granted by ATC to an aircraft to proceed under specified conditions within controlled airspace in order to avoid collisions between known aircraft.

A pilot is not authorized to stray from any rule, regulation, or minimum altitude while under ATC command, nor to perform risky aircraft operations.

ATC facilities will use the terms "ATC clears," "ATC advises," or "ATC requests" to indicate the origin of a clearance, control information, or response to an information request that is given to the pilot via an air-to-ground communication station.

Apron:

The airport apron, sometimes referred to as the apron, flight line, ramp, or tarmac, is the area of an airport where planes are parked, unloaded or loaded, refuelled, boarded, or serviced. Although laws govern its use, such as car lights, the apron is often more accessible to users than the runway or taxiway. The apron, however, is not generally open to the general public, and entry may require a permit. Aircraft stands are the defined areas on an apron for aircraft parking.

The ICAO classifies the apron as part of the mobility area rather than the maneuvering area. On the apron, there are aircraft stand taxi lanes (which provide access to aircraft stands) and apron taxiways (which provide taxi routes across the apron). Apron traffic includes all vehicles, airplanes, and people who use the apron.

Holding Apron

A designated area of an airport where aircraft can wait until the runway is clear. Holding bays, sometimes known as holding aprons, are located near the runways at busy airports.

1. They stop planes before take-off to wait for the runway to clear.
2. The areas are used for aircraft parking before to flight.
3. They are designed in such a way that one aircraft can fly around another whenever necessary.

Holding Instructions.

When an aircraft is cleared to a location other than the destination airport and a delay is foreseen, the ATC controller is responsible for issuing complete holding instructions (unless the pattern is charted), an EFC time, and a best estimate of any extra en route/terminal delay.

If the holding pattern is plotted but the controller does not issue complete holding orders, the pilot is expected to hold as shown on the chart. The controller may delete all holding instructions except the charted holding direction and the sentence as published when the pattern is charted.

Numbering :

Most runways can be used in either direction, depending on the prevailing winds. Furthermore, each runway end is labelled separately. As a result, an aircraft departing on Runway 9-27 from the east is considered to be using Runway 9.

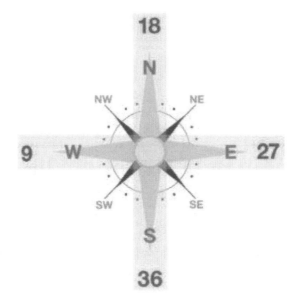

Many large airports have parallel runways, necessitating the identification of an additional runway. For example, Logan International Airport in Boston, Massachusetts, has two parallel runways. Runway 4L-22R is the first, while Runway 4R-22L is the second. When approaching/facing the runway, the letters "L" and "R" denote its relative position (left or right). A few airports have three parallel runways; the runway in the centre is denoted by the letter "C" for centre.

DID YOU KNOW?

Atlanta's Hartsfield-Jackson International Airport (ATL), which serves as Atlanta's major international airport, is the world's second busiest airport in terms of passenger traffic and aircraft movements. It operates 5 runways and handles around 1000 planes per day.

CHAPTER 5

AIRPORT CHARACTERISTICS RELATED TO AIRPORT DESIGN

Airport features are crucial in design since they are formed in terms of knowing amenities to offer for the inhabitants, which is primarily the type of aircraft that is operated.

5.1 Airport Characteristics Related to Airport Design

Airport features are crucial in design since they are formed in terms of knowing amenities to offer for the inhabitants, which is primarily the type of aircraft that is operated.

The features of aircraft have a vital impact in airport layout. The airside and landside planning of the airport are both dependent on the operating characteristics of the aircraft that will be used at the airport. The representative aircraft will measure the runway length and breadth, the minimum separation between runways and taxiways, the geometric project of taxiways, and the pavement strength from the air. Furthermore, environmental issues such as noise and air pollution are predicated on the aircraft that will utilise the airport. The number and size of gates, and hence the terminal architecture, will be influenced by aircraft characteristics in the terminal area.

Finally, the passenger capacity of the aircraft will determine the size of terminal facilities such as passenger lounges and passenger processing systems, as well as the size and kind of baggage handling equipment. Modern aircraft, on the other hand, are projected as a function of the airports where they are meant to operate.

The expenses of adapting an airport to changes in aircraft characteristics, such as runway stretching to accommodate a larger aircraft, have risen so dramatically in recent decades that manufacturers are now cautious about fitting new innovations to old airports. Aircraft are designed with airport facility parameters in mind, such as parking and taxiway size constraints.

Because larger aeroplanes demand more room, modifying the airport configuration is not an option, thus manufacturers are constantly concerned with developing in accordance with it.

5.2 Component Size, Turning Radius, Speed

Turning Radius

Radii of rotation The geometry of an aircraft movement is critical for identifying aircraft position on the apron near to the terminal building and predicting flight paths to other parts of the airport. The nose gear steering angle determines the turning radii. The smaller the radii, the larger the angle. The distances to various sections of the aircraft (wing tips, nose, etc.) form a number of radii from the centre of rotation.

The minimum turning radius data corresponds to the maximum nose gear steering angle provided by the manufacturer, which varies between 60 and 80 degrees. Lesser angles, on the order of 50 or more, are employed to prevent severe tyre wear and, in some cases, scuffing of the tyres.

The turning radius is determined by the kind of aircraft, the wingspan length, and the distance between the rear landing gear. It will be marked with a yellow line on the apron or taxiways, and the pilot will follow the line. It's critical to understand that the aircraft moment is adjusted at a safe distance between planes. During the entry of the aircraft into the apron terminal area, the size of the aircraft will be taken into consideration.

taxiways typically have numerous turning directions, the turning distance and speed are critical. As a result, upon entering the runway, there is a turning radius that can be useful in two categories.

5.3 Types of Entries

- **Conventional 90-degree Taxiway Entry**

Excessive speed during ground manoeuvres might cause the plane to spin out of control, putting the lives of numerous people in jeopardy. That is why, when turning, pilots and air traffic controllers implement speeding limits.

Because it must perform a 90-degree turn via a short-radius curve to line up on the taxiway central line, the aircraft enters the taxiway at a sluggish speed with this style of entry. If take off permission is not received, the aircraft will come to a halt on the taxiway. In this situation, the air traffic controller faces confusion about when the aircraft will take off, thus he or she will normally have provided more than adequate spacing before approving the take off.

- **Typical Rapid Taxiway Entry**

To reduce taxiway occupancy time, the operating technique relies on the usage of rolling take-offs. The taxiway hold line is the same distance from the taxiway central line as the hold line for a traditional 90-degree turn. The safe speed on the curving transition path is the same as it is for high-speed exit. depending on the radius of the turn and the surface conditions.

Speed

The speed of the Aircraft is sometimes crucial on the ground, the ATC is allotted the speed. It must be maintained to avoid the delay. In addition, for the sake of the aircraft's and passengers' safety, a speed will be allocated for certain moments. The speed is indicated on a signboard that is easily understood by pilots at the time of take-off.

The majority of airports do not have a defined taxiing speed limit (though some do). Based on barriers, there is a basic rule for safe speed. There may be limitations imposed by operators and aircraft manufacturers. 20–30 knots (37–56 km/h; 23–35 mph) is a typical cab speed.

High-speed or rapid-exit taxiways are commonly built in congested airports to allow aircraft to leave the runway at higher speeds. This permits the plane to leave the runway faster, allowing another plane to land or take off in less time. This is performed by lowering the angle at which the outgoing taxiway intersects the runway from 90 degrees to 30 degrees, allowing the aircraft to exit the runway at a faster rate.

- **Ground Vehicle speed** :

On any aircraft ramp, no individual operating or driving a vehicle may exceed a speed of 15 miles per hour. When choosing a safe operating speed, factors such as weather and visibility must be considered. the ground vehicle driver must know the signboard and marking.

In the airport, he must drive carefully. The Shuttle buses and ground vehicles, in particular

Component Size

The Airport operations are dependent on aircraft handling, the majority of the components, such as jet bridges, ladder vehicles, trolleys, and other items, must adhere to criteria that are relative to the size of the aircraft.

The parking bays are arranged according to the size of the aircraft and the ground handling vehicle requirements. Occasionally, aeroplanes must be parked for technical maintenance, necessitating more room.

5.4 Airport Characteristics

Airports are divided into two sections: landside and airside. Parking lots, fuel tank farms, and access roads are examples of landside areas. All locations accessible to aircraft, including runways, taxiways, and ramps, are considered airside. At most airports, access from landside to airside is strictly controlled. Commercial flight passengers enter airside areas via terminals, where they can purchase tickets, clear security, check or claim bags, and board aircraft.

Concourses are the waiting spaces that allow passengers to board planes, while this term is frequently used interchangeably with terminal. A ramp is the place where aircraft park near to a terminal to load passengers and luggage. Aprons are aircraft parking zones located distant from terminals.

there are various facility is available in the airport as per the requirement for airline operations, let us go one by understanding how that things to be standardized in the respective to the airport requirements.

AIRFIELD DESIGN

Runway length requirement

For understanding, the runway is created in such a manner that it can match with aircraft takeoff distance and landing. They assume that the aircraft will take off at its maximum takeoff weight from a sea-level airfield on a typical day with no wind and a level runway. As the aforementioned conditions change, the actual runway length required will change. For example, a short-distance flight may not depart with its maximum takeoff weight.

It is highly unlikely that runway length will be restricted due to landing performance. Typically, takeoff runway requirements are greater than landing runway requirements. If a certain aircraft has a greater landing demand, the landing performance will determine the runway need for it.

Runways & Taxiway

The size of the runways and taxiways, as well as the distance between them, is determined by the size of the airport. larger planes for which the airport is intended The airport belongs different types of aircraft. Depending on the size of the aircraft, The more aircraft that will use the airport, the stricter the separation rules will be. the lengths of the runways and taxiways.

Terminal Area

The terminal area is one of the areas of the airport that connects passengers to planes. From airport access to the number of gates, aircraft size and capacity have an impact on practically every aspect of passenger terminal planning. This is crucial because the doors for passenger jet bridges are situated according to the aircraft height, and ground equipment is also set according to the aircraft size and parking space.

There will also be some markings for aircraft parking on the terminal side, which will enable them park in the correct location and connect with other ground equipment.

Apron Area

All aircraft have varied lengths and wingspans, as well as different fuselage sizes and minimum turning radiuses. The aprons are constructed so that the distance between gates is proportional to the wingspan of the aircraft. To save space, airport terminals are typically built with gates of varying sizes, limiting the operations of very big aircraft to a few gates. In order to avoid future levels of congestion, the number and size of gates must be properly calculated.

Airport Fire / Emergency Equipment

The airport's fire emergency equipment is set up in such a way that it can be used quickly to respond to an accident or disaster. The level of protection at an airport is determined by categorizing the airport. The level of protection required is determined by the category to which the airport is designated.

5.5 Capacity and Delay, Factors Affecting Capacity

Capacity

The ability of an airport to accommodate a certain number of traffic is referred to as capacity. As the demand for an airport's services exceeds this limit, queues of people waiting for service form, and they face delays. In general, the larger the demand compared to capacity, the longer the lines and the longer the wait.

The airport is created to meet some form of passengers demand, Every airline determines the timing of operations and even the chosen airport for such operations.

The terms "throughput" and "practical capacity" are frequently used to describe airport capacity. The throughput definition of capacity refers to the speed with which planes can be handled—that is, brought in or out of the airfield without delay. This definition assumes that planes are always available to take off or land, and capacity is measured in terms of how many of these operations can be done in a given length of time. Practical capacity refers to the number of operations (take-offs and landings) that can be accommodated with no more than a given amount of delay (usually stated in terms of maximum tolerated average delay).

Delays

When two or more aircraft seek to use the same runway, taxiway, gate, or other airside facility at the same time, delays develop on the airfield. One must wait while the other is being accommodated. If everyone on the airfield needed service at the same time, the airfield could accommodate everyone at a rate determined solely by the time it took to move them through   the   facilities.

Aircraft, on the other hand, come and depart at a random rate, which implies that even when demand is low compared to capacity, delays might occur. Furthermore, as demand approaches throughput capacity, the likelihood of multiple simultaneous service requests grows rapidly, resulting in an exponential increase in the average delay per aircraft.

Factors Affecting Capacity and Delay

The capacity of an airport varies depending on a variety of physical and operational factors such as airport and airspace design, air traffic control laws and procedures, as well as weather conditions and traffic mix throughout the day or year. In most cases, the average capacity is based on the actual state of the operational experience.

The following are a few reasons that have an important role in flight delays.

- **Characteristics of the Airport**

The runway, taxiways, and aprons are basic determinants of the ability to accept various types of aircraft and the rate at which they can be handled, and the design of the airport elements plays a key part in this. Then there's the equipment that's used for the operations, like as lights, navigational aids, and radar. The sophisticated equipment aids in the smooth and speedy execution of procedures. Types of runway and taxiway designs that take into account the amount of time it takes to connect to the terminal and runway.

- **Airspace Characteristics**

During aircraft operations, the airspace around the airport is being developed further, which can create delays.
Local natural obstacles and built-environment features also have a role in selecting aircraft operations pathways. The position has a direct impact on

79

aviation operations, as it is in an area where flights must land with caution, potentially causing delays.

However, operations at one airport can be impeded when two or more airports are near together. Interfere with each other's operations, lowering acceptance rates at one or both airports or requiring planes to fly around each other to avoid collision. Take, for example, the multiple defense zones and aerodromes that shared the same space.

- **Air Traffic Control**

The fundamental factors of airfield capacity and delay are air traffic control rules and procedures, which are primarily intended to ensure flight safety. The use of parallel or converging runways, aircraft separation, runway occupancy, arrivals and departures spacing, and the use of parallel or converging runways are all laws that can affect overall throughput or cause delays between operations.

- **Meteorological Conditions**

When the weather is clear and visibility is good, airport capacity is normally at its peak. Fog, low ceilings, precipitation, strong winds, or snow or ice accumulations on the runway can severely limit capacity or compel the airport to close. Even a regular occurrence such as a shift in the wind can cause traffic delays while it is rerouted to a new pattern; if the new pattern isn't perfect, capacity can be lowered for as long as the wind blows.

- **Demand Characteristics**

The airport would be crowded with more passengers throughout the summer period, which is a major factor in demand; yet, due to a lack of employees and space, the airport may become even more congested. Capacity and delay are affected by the number of planes that request service, as well as their performance characteristics and how they use the airport. The rate at which they can be handled, as well as any delays that may occur, will be determined by pilot competency.

5.6 Determination **of Runway Capacity Related to Delay**

The number of aircraft movements that can be safely done as defined by aeronautical authorities is referred to as runway capacity. A standard metric of this is the total number of landings and take-offs per hour. Runway. The capacity of a plane is determined by a number of factors, including runway availability, the number of passengers on board, and the plane's size. Operational procedures and meteorological variables such as wind speed and direction, as well as visibility, are all spelled down, as are exits (taxiways connected to the runway).

There are five factors may play role in the delay

Aircraft Separations:

These are the distances between aircraft manoeuvring on runways or in adjacent airspace (which might be stated in terms of time or distance). The main requirement is that an aircraft landing or taking off must have a clean runway in front of it. In order for a following aircraft to take timely evasive action in the event of an accident, certain other separations must be maintained to ensure that this rule is never broken.

Aircraft Characteristics:

The most important factors are weight, speed, and instrumentation. The weight of the aircraft influences wake turbulence separation, whereas speed dictates the time required to fly specified standard separations. The ability to operate in low visibility situations is contingent on the aircraft being outfitted with the proper instrumentation, which works in tandem with the complementary, ground-based equipment deployed on certain runways. Weight and speed both have an impact on runway occupancy periods, and all three may be required to determine if an aircraft may use a certain runway.

The runway's configuration

A runway layout plan essentially has this information. The runway separations and the positions of intersections and exit taxiways are the most important points. Runway lengths and strengths, as well as information about adjacent barriers, are also required if they restrict any aircraft types.

Movement mix

A movement will be described by the type of aircraft, whether it is landing or taking off, as well as the runway on which it occurs. The movement is the sum of the proportions (positive fractions that add up to one) of all the movements indicated by each kind.

Air traffic control strategies

This comprises discretionary policies such as selecting a runway operating mode, giving preference to specific movement types, and deciding whether to alternate landings and take-offs or treat aircraft on a first come, first served basis. Of course, the assertion that these five elements contain all that can affect runway capacity is questionable; yet, it can be shown in the case of a few specific components of airport operations.

5.7 Gate Capacity & Taxiway Capacity

Gate Capacity

The Aircraft gate or Jet bridge is the location where people aboard the aircraft. It is the ideal way for quickly embarking and disembarking aircraft. It also helps airlines boost efficiency for speedy boarding and other tasks performed in the same area. However, Gate is assigned in terms of its aircraft fuselage. A few aircraft have a wide body while others have a narrow body. Adjusting the gate is a challenge to the ground, so certain Pacific airlines with the same type of fleet alter the gate as convenient at the moment, which helps the airline save time and minimize delays. These gates are configured according to airport standards and assigned based on the type of aircraft operations.

It is an enclosed, moveable link that often extends from an airport terminal gate to an airplane, and in some cases from a port to a boat or ship, allowing people to board and leave without walking outdoors and being exposed to inclement weather. A jet bridge may be fixed or moveable, swinging radially and/or expanding in length, depending on building design, sill heights, fuelling stations, and operational requirements.

These gates are subject to availability because they are frequently full during peak times. Few airlines choose to park their planes in the parking bay area, where passengers can be easily connected through shuttle buses from the terminal. Due to preliminary ground tasks and weather, this creates slight delays.

This can be determined by the hourly gate group capacities:

- The no of gates assigned at terminal
- No of wide body gates and narrow body gates.
- Determine the gate mix for each gate group

Taxiway Capacity

As we have know the runway plays an important role in aircraft performance. A few other factors, such as gate capacity and taxiway capacity, also contribute to aircraft delays. Few airports are designed to manage several taxiways for arriving and departing aircraft, with adequate sign marks for directions that readily control traffic and assist other aircraft with landing and takeoff operations. This is especially typical during peak season, when the number of flights at the airport increases. Such delays are common at larger airports.

A taxiway component's capacity is determined as follows:

A. The distance between the end of the runway (the beginning of the takeoff roll) and the taxiway crossing.

B. The runway operations rate, which is the amount of demand that the runway being crossed can accommodate.

C. Few airports have cross runways at this time. When the runway is crossed to accommodate arrivals or mixed operations, the mix index of the runway being traversed is used. When the crossing runway can only accept 90% of departures and touches.

Runway Occupancy Time (ROT).

During an aircraft's arrival, ROT is defined as the time gap between the aircraft crossing the runway's threshold and the tail of the aircraft departing the runway. ROT frequently limits runway capacity since Only one aircraft is permitted to use the runway at any given time. The most crucial The trailing aircraft must first depart the runway and reach the threshold before it may take off.

Conclusion

In conclusion, learning about airport strategic planning has provided valuable insights into the complex and dynamic world of aviation. Understanding the critical elements involved in designing, developing, and managing airports is essential for ensuring safety, efficiency, and sustainability in this vital industry. From capacity management to environmental concerns, security, and passenger experience, strategic planning plays a pivotal role in shaping the future of airports and the broader aviation sector. It highlights the need for a holistic approach that balances the diverse interests of stakeholders while maintaining a focus on the long-term success and resilience of airports in an ever-evolving global landscape.

Reference & Credit:

This chapter extensively explores the fundamental concepts governing the functioning of airports. These concepts draw heavily from the manual of the Federal Aviation Administration (FAA) in the United States, which is widely recognized as the gold standard in best practices. I want to express my gratitude for delivering insightful educational reports. These resources are exclusively intended for educational purposes and serve as a foundational guide for aviation institutes worldwide, illustrating how airports are operated under the oversight of robust aviation authorities.

- FAA guidelines about Runway marking :
  https://www.faa.gov/air_traffic/publications/atpubs/aim_html/chap2_section_3.html
- FAA guidelines about Runway marking:
  https://www.faa.gov/air_traffic/publications
- Airport lights
  https://www.faa.gov/air_traffic/publications/atpubs/aim_html/chap2_section_1.html
  https://s3.amazonaws.com/suncam/docs/417.pdf
- Runway marking
  https://www.faa.gov/air_traffic/publications/atpubs/aim_html/chap2_section_3.html

Made in the USA
Columbia, SC
13 January 2025